KATE LOCK

Kate Lock has always been attracted to new writing as an actress, which inspired her to start writing herself. She co-wrote *Tuesday's Child* with Terry Johnson, playing the lead role for the BBC production, followed by a stage adaptation at Theatre Royal Stratford East. Her other plays include *Job for Life* (Writers' Guild Award), and *Sleeping Dogs*. She has also performed stand-up comedy and written various sketches and monologues.

Film and television work includes the short film *Frank's Bits*, and episodes of *Casualty* for the BBC.

Forthcoming work includes the stage play *Seaview*, and a commission for Radio 4.

Russian Dolls was shortlisted for the 2013 Bruntwood Prize for Playwriting, in association with the Royal Exchange Theatre, Manchester, and won the Adrian Pagan Award, in association with the King's Head Theatre, London.

Kate Lock

RUSSIAN DOLLS

NICK HERN BOOKS

London

www.nickhernbooks.co.uk

A Nick Hern Book

Russian Dolls first published in Great Britain in 2016 as a paperback original by Nick Hern Books Limited, The Glasshouse, 49a Goldhawk Road, London W12 8QP, in association with the King's Head Theatre, London

Cover illustration by Alex Moore
Cover design by Matt Mugan

Designed and typeset by Nick Hern Books, London
Printed in the UK by Mimeo Ltd, Huntingdon, Cambridgeshire PE29 6XX

A CIP catalogue record for this book is available from the British Library

ISBN 978 1 84842 563 7

Russian Dolls was first performed at the King's Head Theatre, London, on 5 April 2016, with the following cast:

HILDA   Stephanie Fayerman
CAMELIA   Mollie Lambert

Director   Hamish McDougall
Designer   Becky-Dee Trevenen
Lighting Designer   Joshua Gadsby
Sound Designer   Max Pappenheim
Assistant Director   Jennifer Davis
Producer   Oscar French

To my patient and trusting agent,
Julia Kreitman

Characters

CAMELIA, *seventeen, vibrant energy*
HILDA, *a strong woman of many years*

This text went to press before the end of rehearsals and so may differ slightly from the play as performed.

Prologue

CAMELIA (*to us*). A bin liner. Fuckin bin liner! Dat's what dey
give me for my stuff. Warden goes to me, 'You never come
inside, wiv no bag of your own.' I go, 'Course I did,
someone must of nicked it.' That proper slows things down
which is not what I want yeah, cos Mum might be waitin
outside the gate. And she never waits for no one. They wait
for her. That's how it goes wiv Mum. Wiv men… Then the
warden, she arks me to sign all da stuff is mine. Like I can
remember? I wanna get out but I ain't goin nowhere wiv no
bin liner. That ain't never a good look. So this Caribbean
warden, she's on da gate, she goes, 'Take you this one, gal.'
It was not my kinda bag, let me tell ya. No way my style.
More like some straw basket wiv pictures of fruit an shit on
da front but she is lookin straight at me. 'Start up ya new
life, new style.' So I go, 'You want me bring it back yeah?'
'Lissen. I don't wanta never see it again. Or you. You get
me?' Then she gives me this proper serious stare. So I nod
ma head and I'm outta there… into the light! Mum wasn't
pickin up and she weren't nowhere to be seen outside da
gates. She ain't got no car!… but that's how it come up, in
my head, in colour, wiv music yeah. Mum, drivin up in some
stylish BMW wiv da roof off yeah and Beyoncé like blarin
out… And she brakes sudden like and leans over to open da
door wiv a tray a doughnuts on da back and her in some new
bikini cos we ain't goin home, nah, we drivin to da coast,
meet her new friends wiv wine coolers an beach houses, an
an… But I'm still standin here wiv my fruit bag, don't know
for how long. Then I see Alice, my key social. Her like
wavin across the traffic tryin get my attention.

Darkness except on HILDA*'s face.*

HILDA (*to us*). It happened just like that, Tommy Cooper style.
I was having my bath, dinner in the oven. Toad in the hole.

Onion gravy. Lovely. So, I'm in the bath, getting hungry, head against the taps, I never slouch in case I drop off so the taps are there to keep me focused on the job. There's a lot to wash these days, under the folds. It's like a geography lesson, all those terraces for growing rice, or was it tea? From the top down to sea level in India or was it China? Then I look up out the window and I can see next door's silver birch, waving in and out of the frame, like it was dancing with someone it didn't want to let go of. That's the very last thing I see.

The lights come up on HILDA*'s full body.*

Tried to open my eyes but they were already open. I tried to get out of the bath but I slipped and knocked myself out. Didn't know if I'd come round, or if I was dead. Till I could smell my burning dinner. It was like I'd come to the end of the story but I was still in it.

Lights down on HILDA. *Up on* CAMELIA.

CAMELIA (*to us*). So Alice goes to me she's bringin me straight from the Young Offenders to some new hostel. Not home. Not allow. There've been developments. Hate that word. It's not houses like you'd think. New homes on some estate not quite finished. Fuckin developments... Mum's only gone an let Troy come back so they've had to remove the little 'uns and keep me away. Alice goes, 'It would be inadvisable to visit your mum' but I don't spar wiv her. I mean... What a fuckin job! No one likes a social, I mean no one. What I can't believe is they went university an got some degree to get a shit job like that. And her nails! When there's no nail left, she like bites the skin on the outside. Eats it. She don't touch the biscuits. She's the one who's mental.

Lights down on CAMELIA. *Up on* HILDA.

HILDA (*to us*). You try callin nine-nine-nine with your eyes shut! And naked. Couldn't find my clothes so I grabbed what felt like a towel or two and covered meself best I could, groping my way to the front door. Was it night or day? All I knew was I had to get myself somehow on the 431. I started shouting but nothing came back, then this Indian chappie drops out of nowhere and saves my bacon. We're on the bus and I don't let go of his arm. He takes off his coat and wraps it round me. Tells me he's got a better one at home. Sees me off, and in to reception at Moorfields. Tells me I'm in good hands now or was it God's hands? It took the doctor less than an hour to tell me there's nothing they could do. Very nice about it he was. Nice as he could be when you think about it. Everyone was nice except me. It took me six months to get out of bed, stop feeling sorry for myself. I wouldn't answer the phone. Couldn't see the point. Then my mum's voice started in my head one morning. She knocked some sense in there. Got me on my feet. My first day back at the day centre, we all managed a laugh about it. You have to. Audrey'd gone and lost her left leg since I went blind. Diabetes. Like it was all part of the big joke called life. Wanted to know if I'd like to swap. Her eyes for my leg. I'm still thinking about it.

Lights down on HILDA.

Scene One

We hear a few bars of classical Spanish music; Adagio from Concierto de Aranjuez.

Lights up on HILDA*'s kitchen/living room. Furniture sparse, with soft corners and devices for the blind. There are photos of children and primitive kids' paintings all over the walls.*

HILDA *juices lemons and measures sugar as she listens. At a crescendo moment, she suddenly lifts her arms, twisting her wrists like a flamenco dancer, her chest thrust out with pride.*

There is a loud knock. She navigates her way confidently to the record player, turns down the volume. A second knock. She approaches the closed door avoiding furniture.

HILDA. That you, Lorraine? Bit early.

CAMELIA (*off*). Nah. She's not comin. Sorry. Different one today. Can I come in?

HILDA. Agency never phoned. They usually phone if there's…

CAMELIA (*off*). Not my fault, lady. Look I got ID 'n' that…

HILDA. Lot of good that is to me. I'll call them now.

HILDA *moves away from door.*

CAMELIA (*off*). Listen, lady, I ain't got time to hang about. Mrs Hilda Porter yeah?

HILDA. Last time I checked.

CAMELIA (*off*). You better let me in now else I won't have time. You get me… You need help yeah? To get you to bed 'n' dat.

HILDA. Bed? It's half-past five.

CAMELIA (*off*). I got six more to fit in after you. That's why I come early.

HILDA *opens the door.* CAMELIA *enters, in jogging pants with hair scraped back.* HILDA *closes the door.*

You want me to tidy up or what? Not sayin it needs it. I seen a lot worse than this yeah.

HILDA *squares up to her.*

HILDA. How do I know you ain't a murderer?

CAMELIA. I go to church innit.

HILDA. So did Henry the Eighth and that never stopped him.

CAMELIA. Who?

HILDA. You English?

CAMELIA. You racist?

HILDA. Another chippy one. Is that why Lorraine's not come. She's got the ump with me over her buyin the wrong lard.

HILDA *moves slowly back to the kitchen table and measures sugar, etc.* CAMELIA *has a good look around the room.*

CAMELIA. She's down wiv flu. You want me to like run you a bath?

HILDA. Everyone washes too much these days. You can cut up them lemons. Get the pips out. I'm making lemonade. You can have some if you're good.

CAMELIA. Got any Coke?

HILDA. No. What do I call you?

CAMELIA. Camelia.

HILDA. Like the flower?

CAMELIA. Dunno.

HILDA. There's one out the back. Blossoms twice a year. Hope you manage it more than that.

CAMELIA. You only got me an hour. You want me go down the shops?

HILDA. Do you chew gum all the time?

CAMELIA. Stops me from smokin. Stunts your growth innit.

HILDA. You need to grow?

CAMELIA. What does it look like!

HILDA. I don't know, dear, I can't see you.

CAMELIA. What!… what like not at all?

HILDA. I can tell light from dark.

CAMELIA. Like blind, like completely? I knew you was old but I never… shit I never… That's terrible. The agency shoulda… I mean if I was blind I'd like… fuckin ell!

HILDA. Yes it came as a bit of a shock to me too.

CAMELIA. Sorry for swearin but… Shit. Can't they give you some operation?

HILDA. No. There's nothing they can do.

CAMELIA. You shoulda gone private. If I was blind, I wouldn't even get out of bed.

HILDA. I didn't. For six months. Then I had my epiphany.

CAMELIA. Operation?

HILDA. No, Mum's voice. 'There's nothing about you not to like, and loads that you should love.'

CAMELIA. Even your hair?

HILDA. What's wrong with my hair? Oona does it for me Fridays down the centre.

CAMELIA. Just cos you're blind don't mean you have to have it flat. You could lift it wiv some layerin and product, give it some shape, some style, yeah.

HILDA. What you doing in a care agency? Hope you've done your training?

CAMELIA. I got paperwork somewhere. Read it out loud if ya like?

CAMELIA *finds nothing in her pockets except a bin liner.*
HILDA *dismisses the idea with a wave of the hand.*

HILDA. Before I forget, can you pick up them empties by the sink, put them on the doorstep for the milkman in the morning.

CAMELIA. Is that cos you is blind?

CAMELIA *picks up milk bottles and goes to door.*

HILDA. Where've you been living?

CAMELIA. Glebe Estate. Lucky you never have to see that shithole.

CAMELIA *places bottles outside…*

I don't get it. Da full ones will get nicked innit?

HILDA. People are more honest than you think.

CAMELIA. No they ain't. Why you not like safe in some home?

CAMELIA *picks up bin liner again and surveys the room.*

HILDA. Goddaughter was all for me moving in with her. Basingstoke. They think cos you're blind it don't matter where they put you.

CAMELIA *picks up* HILDA*'s handbag.*

Don't move anything!

CAMELIA *freezes as if caught out.*

Not even an inch. I know where everything is, and that's how it stays. Lose my bearings... lose my mind.

CAMELIA *carefully removes the purse from the bag and puts it in the bin liner as she chats.*

CAMELIA. What's it like bein blind?

HILDA. Fill that jug up to the two-pint mark, will you?

CAMELIA *obliges.*

CAMELIA. Why you makin lemonade? Why don't I get you some down Londis?

HILDA. I'd rather eat my own leg than swallow that stuff.

HILDA *continues preparing the lemonade.*

You walk into a lift and...

CAMELIA. What lift?

HILDA. You asked me what it's like?... So you're in a lift. It's as if you're going up to the top floor, all on your own, only you keep going up beyond that, up into space. And then when it stops at last, the doors open and you step out into... into nothing. Oblivion.

CAMELIA. I'd shoot myself.

CAMELIA *continues to steal ornaments, vases, shoes, quietly watching and conversing with* HILDA *as she does so.*

HILDA. Have to convince yourself, you're not gonna fall over, then you don't. Sometimes I get a sudden urge to do a handstand.

CAMELIA. Don't let me stop ya...

HILDA. I'm not wearing my best knickers.

CAMELIA. How do you know?

HILDA. Got my system. Have to log every detail in my box –
(*Taps her head.*) and remember. Outside is a lot worse than
in here.

CAMELIA. What's all dem plastic bits on your furniture?

CAMELIA *protects the breakables in tea towels.*

HILDA. The OT come round and took anything that could kill
me. Then I got fitted with bleepers, pingers, railings… I put
up a real fight when they come to take away my cooker. Had
that stove thirty years. I'm a proper cook see.

CAMELIA. You been on the telly?

HILDA. Two hundred and fifty mouths to feed in that canteen
every day on one-and-sixpence luncheon vouchers. Soup,
main and always a dessert. The men used to call me Queen
of the Puddings. What you doing over there?

CAMELIA. Ah dese little dolls are well dusty. Nice yeah but
you buy em budget?

HILDA. My goddaughter brought them back from the Black
Sea. Hand-painted.

As she slips them into the bin liner she talks loudly.

CAMELIA. No they ain't. They got the same mistake on each
of em. Like some smudge. Can't paint da same mistake by
hand again and again. Cept da baby. She's so liccle you can't
see. (*Seeing photos on wall.*) Dey like your grandchildren?
Got bare loads of em.

HILDA. So long as they're not your own, kids are alright.

CAMELIA. You some teacher?

HILDA. Me a teacher? Ha! I trained as a cook first. Proper one.
Then I was a mum. Foster-mum.

CAMELIA. Should of had some of your own. Dey might be
lookin after ya now.

The sound of a pinger.

HILDA. Only bleedin thing they'll let me use. Some idiot-proof apology for an oven.

HILDA *gets out a plastic loaf tin from the oven.*

Smells about right. Doreen give me some windfalls at the day centre. You like apple cake?

CAMELIA. Don't do fruit.

HILDA. Why don't you take out that horrible gum and try some.

CAMELIA. Nah. I'm alright.

HILDA. That's rude. You could of pretended. Wouldn't have known would I?

CAMELIA *unhooks a clock from the wall and gets it down. Then she takes some vinyl records.*

What you got there?

CAMELIA. Thought I'd empty your bins like I said.

HILDA. So long as you don't empty my fridge like Lorraine. Silly cow with her sell-by dates. What else is a nose for? Open this can of pilchards for me. Awkward bugger but I love em for me tea.

CAMELIA. Can't. I got nails yeah. I can do ya toast before I go.

HILDA. You only just got here.

HILDA *proffers the pilchard tin.* CAMELIA *doesn't take it.*

CAMELIA. How come you gotta cook so much?

HILDA. I told you, it's my purpose in life... (*Opening the can.*) What's yours?

CAMELIA. Look I gotta go check anuvver one. She'll get proper vex if I'm late. What you doin? Stop it. You're bleedin... Look!

HILDA. Where there's a will...

CAMELIA. Why can't you have baked beans like everyone else? Look, lady, I gotta go.

HILDA. Clear off then but I'm not paying for an hour.

HILDA persists with the can. She is bleeding.

CAMELIA. Lissen yeah! You gotta stop that now. You've got blood like drippin on your apron...

HILDA. That's what it's for. Should of seen the blood on me when I was working Smithfields. A lot easier jointing a lamb than this bugger.

CAMELIA. You're mad you are. Euch!

CAMELIA takes can from her and puts it in the swing bin. She grabs a clean tea towel and wraps it round HILDA's hand.

Keep still will ya.

A mobile ringtone. Classical.

HILDA. Get that will you, first shelf, before it rings off. Where you put my pilchards?

CAMELIA picks up the mobile but hesitates, instead of answering she hands it to HILDA.

CAMELIA. You should get a doctor yeah. Proper one stitch that up.

CAMELIA grabs her bin liner of loot and exits.

HILDA. Yes... Oh Lorraine, I'm sorry you're poorly... poorly... not well...

HILDA hears the door close.

Camelia? Camelia!

HILDA back on the mobile.

She never even said goodbye... the new one they sent stead of you... Camelia... no, but I like her pluck... pluck, never mind... what do you mean?... You sure?... But she... No, I don't think she... you better come and see. Why would she...

HILDA stops. She looks around her without seeing. Her hand still bleeding.

Scene Two

CAMELIA s*moking, wired.*

CAMELIA (*to us*). When I hand over da cash to Yussef he goes to me, 'Dat ain't enough.' I watched him slide dem notes down the front of his jeans. I could jus see his beautiful scar. He looks at me like I'm not dere, like I ain't trappin for him bare stacks. He should be like… I dunno like… nice or somink. Den Henry starts on about what a liccle girl I am, an Yussef should try it. Like he bin dere, an that's a lie! I ain't never bin wiv Henry. (*Spits*.) But he's makin it like we was sweet, winkin at me an nudgin Yussef like he's ma pimp an dat. Shit. I ain't got no respec for Henry.

She stubs out her fag.

Before I know it, dey is all movin in on me, sniffin and jokin and lookin at me… My bruvver Zach's dere, outside da door but I can see him. He could have got me out of it. (*Stops. Bites her lip*.) But dat's my bruvver, he don't say nuffink till he has to. And den, no one respec him enough to lissen.

Lights down on CAMELIA. *Up on* HILDA, *wrist bandaged.*

HILDA (*to us*). They come round. Two uniforms, asking me for a description! Can you credit it? I couldn't even tell em what she'd pinched. Never felt so useless. That's what's got to me. Not the stuff, I can live without that. Bit of a nuisance getting my jacket back from the dry cleaner's, mind. The ticket was in my purse that she took. Without the ticket I don't know whose jacket I've come home with. She pinched my new flamenco shoes 'n' all. For classes up the centre. Why did she do that?

Lights down on HILDA. *Up on* CAMELIA.

CAMELIA (*to us*). My bruvver give me a lift. After they finished wiv me. I didn't know where we was goin but he parks right by our church. Where we used to go when we was kids, cept nah dere's no one in dere. He sits me down in a pew, then he goes an nicks some white flower outta some vase on the altar and gives it to me. A real flower. Never says nuffink. Never does. Then he's gone… I sit there, holdin my flower and starin at the white cloths and candles. Cash bitch is all dey want. I can't make it on the outside no more! I know dat nah.

Lights down on CAMELIA.

Lights up on HILDA*'s living room. We hear a van driving off before* HILDA *enters, hand bandaged. She closes door behind her and walks into the room. Sensing something, she stops.* CAMELIA *emerges from the bathroom.*

(*To* HILDA.) How's your hand?

HILDA *jumps but tries to control her fear.*

HILDA. How the hell…?

CAMELIA. I shoulda sorted you out myself. I coulda done dat.

HILDA. Get out of here now.

CAMELIA. Don't look so scared.

HILDA *fumbles and tries to press an alarm around her neck.*

HILDA. I mean it. The warden is on his way.

CAMELIA. Good. I broke in fru da bathroom winda. Tell him get da feds yeah. I'll make us tea while we waitin.

A pool of water on the floor emerges from between HILDA*'s legs…* CAMELIA *goes to put the kettle on.*

Oh my god you wet yourself. Oh my god, I ain't gonna harm ya I'm makin you a cuppa tea. Would I do that if I was gonna cut ya? That ain't my style, not unless my blood's up. Like that bitch got me done. She was proper arksin for it but I don't make no cuppa tea first.

HILDA. No one robs me! Do you hear?

CAMELIA. I did.

HILDA. No one!

HILDA *moves boldly towards her and lashes out with her white stick in* CAMELIA*'s direction but misses, loses her balance and falls to the ground.*

CAMELIA. Easy yeah. You wanna hand up?

HILDA. Pass me my stick.

> CAMELIA *puts the stick in her hand.* HILDA *strikes her across the back.*

CAMELIA. Ow! What you do that for? I'm makin ya tea.

HILDA. I don't want tea I want you to get out of my house!

> HILDA *emphatically strikes her stick against the table.*

> Now! Or I'll give you the hiding you deserve.

> CAMELIA *is chastened. She makes for the door.*

CAMELIA. You better chill, lady. I come back laters.

HILDA. You stay away from me if you know what's good for you!

> CAMELIA *opens the door. Hesitates. She slams the door but remains on the inside watching* HILDA, *who shudders with relief. She sets off to the bathroom.* CAMELIA *sees* HILDA *is about to fall over her bin liner.*

CAMELIA. Wait! Stop!…

> HILDA *turns.* CAMELIA *comes to move her bin liner.*

> I don't want ya like fallin over again. It's all your stuff yeah.

> CAMELIA *puts items back, including Russian dolls…*

> Reckon you'd want it back what I couldn't shift? Like dis clock don't work but don't spose dat worries ya. Turkish down the pawn shop was proper rude about these liccle wooden dolls, an I think dey is lovely. He goes 'lovely' got nuffink to do wiv value. An I thought he was like just bein Turkish yeah but the uvver shop, he was proper harsh. I won't tell you what he said.

> HILDA *makes for her mobile.*

> An what about I use dis tray for tea innit.

HILDA. I don't care what your excuses are. I don't give a thrupenny fuck what happens to you, I'm calling the police.

CAMELIA. Go on yeah. Da feds, da social, da warden. Bring it on. All of em yeah.

HILDA. Hope they cut off your thievin hands.

CAMELIA. 'Kin hell. Dat's not very nice.

HILDA. That'd soon learn you. But they won't. They'll give you a tickin off and take you to Alton bleedin Towers.

CAMELIA. Legoland. Dat's where we fetched up last time, but it rained all day. Go on call em. Don't let me stop ya. You can use my mobile.

HILDA. People, proper working people pay taxes to keep scum like you afloat.

CAMELIA. They don't have to.

HILDA. They do. It's called the law but you wouldn't know about that, you shameless mare.

CAMELIA. You gonna report me or what? Then you can get shotta me, back inside where I belong.

HILDA (*on phone*). Hello?… No… emergency services.

HILDA *fumbles with the phone again then waits for a voice.*

CAMELIA. That's all I want, lady. Proper safe again inside the Young Offenders. I'll get my social Alice on da line. She'll get da feds on it if you tell her what I done.

HILDA. Why don't you tell her yourself?

CAMELIA. She won't believe me. Reckons I'm like all reformed since I come out da YOI.

CAMELIA *taps a number on her mobile and puts it in* HILDA*'s hand.*

It's ringin. You got every right. I robbed ya I broke in, an I lied. They got a proper name for dat.

HILDA. Got a receipt or did you steal this as well?

CAMELIA. My mate give it me if you wanna know. Her bruvver works Currys. But you can tell the feds I nicked it

yeah. Big it up. They'll believe a nice old lady like you…
cept you ain't nice.

CAMELIA *approaches but* HILDA *stiffens.*

HILDA. It's another trick.

HILDA *launches mobile across the room.* CAMELIA
screams and runs after it. HILDA *moves towards her
landline phone.*

CAMELIA. The face is cracked! I could do ya for damage. Leila
never said you was a nutter. I can't believe you done dat!

HILDA *stops when she hears the name.*

HILDA. Leila? Not my Leila?

CAMELIA. She said you was fam. Best she ever had, but that
ain't sayin much. You lucky it's workin.

HILDA. Where is she?

CAMELIA. We shared, inside. Goes to me, like you was her
gran, till I found out you wasn't. She told me, come find ya,
show ya dis photo. I got it on my phone. She never said you
was blind.

HILDA. I could see back then. Tell me straight… Did Leila set
you up to rob me?

CAMELIA. Nah! She proper loves ya. Don't know why when
you's so harsh.

HILDA *drops into a chair, greatly relieved. Her head in her
hands. She might be laughing or crying it is hard to tell.*
CAMELIA *finds the photo on her mobile.*

It's a picture of her kid. Chad, he's called, after the
desert where his dad come from. He's bare cute. Shame
you can't see.

HILDA. Leila's got a kid?… Inside?

CAMELIA. Nah. Chad's living wiv his auntie till Leila's done
her stretch. She wanted you to know like you bein fam 'n' dat.

HILDA. So why doesn't she call me? They got phones inside.

CAMELIA. Maybe she thinks you'll kick off like you done jus nah. Your warden's takin his time. If I was some murderer you'd be well dead by nah.

HILDA. I miss that girl. You should of said straight off you knew Leila. Why didn't you?

CAMELIA. I was fleecin ya innit.

HILDA. I'd of given you anything you wanted. A friend of Leila's.

CAMELIA. Cash is what I needed… It's too late nah. I'll get my social, an you can tell her what I done, get me back inside yeah.

CAMELIA *tries the number again. Engaged. She recognises Leila's photo on the wall.*

Dat's her alright. Dem big black eyes.

HILDA. Was she dealing?

CAMELIA. She got stitched up. Took da rap for dem uvvers what got away.

HILDA. She needs a lot that gel. Are they helping her inside…?

CAMELIA. They're on it like no one else. Every minute. And you get to proper know da staff. Like Leila an me we're like eatin, at some big table, like puddins an dat, every day. Then we wash up and no one is bunkin off or flippin out at ya. And dey listen if you got some issue you wanna 'explore' dat's what they call it. Stacks of time for dat. Like we done papier mâché and masks of someone we know. I done my dad. I made him up. When it was finished, the tutor puts it up on da wall, well embarrassin. Anuvver time some actors showed, like budget ones. Never been on telly or nuffink. Leila was goin on an on about it, sayin like I shoulda watched em, so I reckon next time I'll go wiv her. An I'll tell her she gotta call you yeah.

CAMELIA *checks phone again. Engaged.*

Alice must be gassin wiv her boyfriend like forever. She feels too much is her problem, like she goes to me, she wanna give me a proper hug, only she never dare. There's like no one watchin us, an I swear I won't report her if she hugs me, but she's like, 'I can't take da risk,' so she can keep her fuckin hug.

HILDA *doesn't move.* CAMELIA *explores cupboards. Prepares tea.*

Bet you got a teapot somewhere. My mum keeps hers in da box it come in. Never gets it out. I don't know what she's waitin for. She never even got it out for Destiny's christenin. (*Finds teapot.*) Ahh. That's so pretty. I want one of dem when I…

HILDA. How old are you?

CAMELIA. Seventeen. Whenever I open a fridge at the hostel, dere is no milk… not what you could drink. When I get my flat I'm gonna have a man deliver like you. Or a cow. A cow in my front room yeah.

HILDA. You won't be going to no Young Offenders unit now, young lady.

CAMELIA. Who's gonna stop me?

HILDA. The day you turn eighteen you're an adult.

CAMELIA. But I ain't.

HILDA. I know that, but they don't. In the eyes of the law when you reach eighteen you jump from child to woman.

CAMELIA. But I'm only seventeen. Some a da gals inside are twenty-one I swear so I'm safe.

HILDA. Do you really think they're keeping your bed warm for you?

CAMELIA. Shit!

CAMELIA *paces like a caged animal.*

I can't… you don't know… It's the only… Three times a week, one to one… I'm like important. And then they go and cut my sentence!

HILDA. If you get done again custodial, they could bang you up somewhere serious… You can forget your papier mâché.

CAMELIA*'s mobile starts to ring. She checks it but doesn't answer.*

CAMELIA. It's Alice. Shit! I don't know what to tell her nah… I can't do da outside no more … There's stuff goin on… I can't…

CAMELIA *is struggling with the reality of her situation.*

HILDA. Why isn't your mum sorting you out? She banged up 'n' all?

CAMELIA. You know nuffink about my mum so shut up.

HILDA. Twenty-three years of fostering I come across one decent responsible mother, and she was from Bangladesh. They give birth to you, then they mess you up for the rest of us to pick up the pieces.

CAMELIA*'s mobile rings again.*

I'll talk to your social worker. Give it here.

CAMELIA. You gonna shop me?

HILDA. You robbed me.

CAMELIA. Only cos I had to get some cash to em.

HILDA. Who? Who are they?

CAMELIA *picks up.*

CAMELIA.…In college… No… I'm there now I swear… well she's… register?… Nah, she must of got me mixed up wiv da uvver midget. You rinsin m'llowance… I gotta go.

She finishes call. Continues to make tea.

HILDA. Mean as you are with the truth, I hope you can save some for yourself.

CAMELIA. We can have it nice on a tray like at one of my meetins. I've had more meetins than the fuckin Prime Minister. Plastic cups and dem shit-stirrers but...

HILDA. You still owe me. What are you going to do about that?

CAMELIA. I'm makin you tea innit!

CAMELIA *finds shortbread and scoffs.*

HILDA. What did you get banged up for?

CAMELIA. I ain't killed no one if that's what you're thinkin an I'm not stupid. Counsellor inside says I've got a lot goin for me. I could have a future.

HILDA. I've had one of them.

CAMELIA. Gotta build up some CV. Like uvver stuff you done what ain't on your police record. So now I gotta do some uvver stuff... You wanna sit here or watch telly?

HILDA. What do you think?

CAMELIA. Oh my god where's your telly?

HILDA. I'm losing patience here. If you don't tell me the truth, Camelia, I'll get you sent down somewhere they check your arsehole for drugs and feed you cabbage stew in a bucket.

CAMELIA. I got into a fight in care alright! Mclanic, greedy bitch. We was in da kitchen an she goes, 'I love Coco Pops' and I was like... no you don't. Then she goes yeah she proper loves em, but I said she can't love Coco Pops, she can only *like* them, cos for a start they can't love her back. It's not like lovin God or your mum. Then she goes 'Your mum is jus the same as Coco Pops she never loves you back. Your mum is some junky whore.' So I nutted her. Wiv da kettle... Jus boiled.

HILDA. Sweet Jesus.

CAMELIA. She should never have said dat. Don't know what I'll do if I see her again.

HILDA. You upset cos it was true?

CAMELIA *freezes with the teapot in her hand.*

Your mum can't get off the gear or the game or both? But the courts give her the benefit? Every one of those kids up there on the wall was waiting for the same as you.

CAMELIA. Shut up.

HILDA. Gary – (*Points to his picture.*) five years old when he came to me. Looked about three. Thought it was all his fault she couldn't love him like she should.

CAMELIA *approaches, almost threatening* HILDA *with the teapot in her hand.* HILDA *unaware.*

So scared he was of his own mother, I'd find him sleeping under the bed at night in case he wet the mattress. Not a word out of him for three months till I won him round.

CAMELIA. You know nuffink about it! I swear you got no right…

CAMELIA *close to* HILDA *with the teapot. It looks dangerous.*

HILDA. No rights! True enough. She had all the rights in court. Won him back, her property… Just long enough to teach him a few more shades of fear.

CAMELIA. That's enough!

HILDA. What? I never understood that. How you can own a child.

CAMELIA. Enough I said. Enough.

CAMELIA *stops herself from scalding* HILDA. *Slams down the teapot and storms out.*

HILDA. You and your big mouth, Hilda.

She swings her stick in frustration, almost smashing the teapot.

Blackout.

Scene Three

CAMELIA (*to us*). 'You don't get anyfink for nuffink in dis world.' Dat's my mum, an she's right. Anyfink budget, she won't touch. Never took us to no parks cos dey was free, an she's got class. She's like savin up take us Disney, not Paris, proper lame, but LA innit. (*Pause*.) She don't pick up when I call, an I ain't allow ta visit cos a Troy… it's not like he's gonna fiddle wiv me. My mum's boyfriends never touch me. She goes I'm safe wiv em, no danger, the way I look. When I was in care dat time it was da same. Musta been like da only kid what wasn't fiddled wiv. So I never got no presents. Like Chelsea got make-up to keep her mouth shut. (*Pause*.) Troy ain't no paedo he's worse. Careless prick leavin his works around da flat. Some new social on a visit, she sees my little sista playin wiv his syringe an she goes mental. (*Pause*.) Mum swears she gonna kill herself if they don't let her have her liccle ones back. I know who I wanna kill. (*Pause*.) Since Mum let Troy come back my bruvver Zach, he ain't got no time for her. 'Keep away from her, from da crew, from everyone, includin me.' Dat's the most words I ever got from my bruvver. (*Pause*.) Should of lissened… but I never.

Lights down on CAMELIA.

Lights up. HILDA'*s kitchen/living area. Evening. Weeks later. Spanish music. Large cardboard boxes on the floor.* HILDA *is climbing up a stepladder. It looks dangerous as she steadies herself for a moment. She feels around the frame of a kid's picture* (Gary) *on the wall, and removes it, nearly losing her balance. Her mobile rings. She answers.*

HILDA. Ruth… No… I've got my feet up… I've told you I'm stopping where I am… You can't… Norman told me at the centre it's an infringement of my human rights… until I'm potty… Feet first, dear, that's the only way you'll get me to Basingstoke…

A loud banging at the door.

CAMELIA (*off*). Hilda!

HILDA. If you do… you'll be wasting your time, dear. (*Finishes call.*)

CAMELIA (*off*). Let me in! Hilda!… Hilda! Please. You gotta let me in.

HILDA. You walked out on me. That ain't happening again.

HILDA *drops the picture frame to the ground*

CAMELIA. What was that? I can make ya tea an toast. I can sort ya winda.

HILDA. Been fixed a fortnight, now bugger off.

CAMELIA. If you don't let me in I'm gonna throw myself in the canal.

HILDA. Go on then.

HILDA *makes her way down the ladder.*

You still there? Camelia?

Some sad garden flowers are squeezed through the letter box in the door.

What you up to?

CAMELIA. You gotta get em in water yeah. I could do it. I'm not feelin well. Just let me in… for a glass of water yeah?

HILDA *can hear* CAMELIA *in tears.*

HILDA. How do I know you're not pretending?

HILDA *opens the door.* CAMELIA *enters breathless, hair a mess.*

You drunk? I can smell vodka.

CAMELIA. It's in my hair. I never drank none I swear.

CAMELIA *puts a small heavy package wrapped in a blue plastic bag under the sofa before she gulps some water.* HILDA *stays by the door.*

HILDA. I can smell a fella in this.

CAMELIA. You smashin stuff up on purpose?

HILDA. You'll find the dustpan under the sink.

CAMELIA *obeys. She checks at the window that no one has followed her.*

CAMELIA. And you ain't even dressed yet. You movin out?

HILDA. Not if I can help it. Just getting rid of stuff. What's your game?

CAMELIA *is clearing the debris.*

CAMELIA. Da frame's broke but I'll put his picture here by yer radio yeah. I gotta eat somink.

HILDA. Bananas in the bowl.

CAMELIA. Don't do bananas.

HILDA. Then you can't be hungry. Whoever he is I hope you took precautions.

CAMELIA. What? Shut up. It weren't like that.

HILDA. Like what?

CAMELIA. No. It wasn't… I proper need a fix of somethin.

HILDA. Did he hurt you?

CAMELIA. No. It's my bruvver, Zach. You got any fags?

HILDA. Someone's hurt him?

CAMELIA *grabs a banana. She bites. She gags on it.*

If you're not going to tell me, then why did you come?

CAMELIA. You got any drugs? All old ladies got pills.

HILDA. Do we need to get help to your brother?

CAMELIA *covers her face.*

I'll get you something soon as you're straight with me.

CAMELIA. I can't tell ya. It's too…

HILDA. Did you hurt someone?

CAMELIA. I couldn't get out of it. I swear. You won't believe it. Like no one would. What I done… I feel so dirty I wanna die. Right now. Cept I'll go straight to hell but I didn't have no choice.

HILDA *reaches for her hand*. CAMELIA *withdraws it*.

I blew him didn't I. My own bruvver. They made me.

HILDA. Who are they?

CAMELIA. On my knees. Dem all watchin… Henry goes to me, if I don't give him head, my own bruvver, he's gonna blaze him. At first I thought he was gassin, but like he puts a gun to my bruvver's nuts and Zach fixes me wiv dem eyes an goes, 'They're bluffin, sis. Don't do it, sis, don't,' but I'm like starin at dis shooter in Henry's hand pointin at my bruvver's dick, and beads of sweat comin off Zach's nose. (*Pause. Tries to hold back tears.*) Then Henry goes to me… 'If you don't take hold of your bruvver's dick, I gonna post it cross da manor first-class mail in little pieces.' So I… I…

CAMELIA *crumbles in shame on the floor*. HILDA *reaches down to her*.

HILDA. Come here.

CAMELIA. What you doin?

HILDA *on her knees. She pulls* CAMELIA *in towards her bosom. She closes her arms around her tight into a long slow embrace*. HILDA *cradles and strokes her head*.

HILDA. You could do with a bit more of this than the other.

CAMELIA. Don't stop.

HILDA. You're in the wrong soil, Camelia. Got to get you out of the shade.

HILDA *continues to stroke her head*.

If you're ever going to blossom. But first we have to report this.

CAMELIA *breaks the embrace*.

CAMELIA. Like I'm gonna grass up my bruvver's crew.

HILDA. We'll leave him out of it.

CAMELIA. He's tight wiv em. They're all sworn.

HILDA. Animals! All of em. If I had my way I'd have them all castrated. Publicly. I'm calling the police.

As HILDA *moves,* CAMELIA *stops her.*

You'll let them get away with it?

CAMELIA. Less you wanna see me scarred or worse… You get me? No feds! I didn't wanna tell ya. I didn't wanna come here. I jus wanna forget it yeah.

HILDA. Why did you come here? Why not go to your mum's?

CAMELIA. Cos if Troy answers the door I'll fuckin kill him!

HILDA. Why doesn't she get rid of him?

CAMELIA. Cos she fuckin loves him.

HILDA. More than her kids?

CAMELIA *paces, restless. She checks outside the window.*

CAMELIA. You wanna rubbish her like da social but she can't help herself. She's proper fit and men don't leave her alone. You'd never believe she is my muvver. Serious. Her legs, her shoes…

HILDA. She ever cook for you?

CAMELIA. No one cooks no more. You're the weirdo. I had a mate, primary. Her mum cooked stuff every day. I don't know how she put up wiv it. You got any Bacardi?

HILDA. Your mum visit you when you was inside?

CAMELIA. She wasn't well. She has to sleep daytime.

HILDA. Don't tell me she's another addict?

CAMELIA. No she's a fuckin ballerina!

CAMELIA *starts to look in cupboards.*

HILDA. I got some cooking sherry. You can have a tipple when you peel the spuds.

CAMELIA *finds and knocks back sherry from the bottle*.

CAMELIA. You don't get me. You're wastin yer time.

HILDA. Then why did you come?

CAMELIA. Dunno.

HILDA. I think you do.

CAMELIA. Whatever! I'm goin nah innit. Gotta see my little bruvver an sister where dey fostered before it's too late. Bring em some crisps.

CAMELIA *searches in cupboard for crisps*.

HILDA. You can't just turn up without warning. Not fair on the family. There's procedure.

CAMELIA. Gotta see em before dey get adopted. Everyone's got crisps. Don't tell us you make your own?

HILDA. Don't go! Please. I've made a pie we can stretch between us with gravy and spuds.

CAMELIA. I can't peel no fuckin potatoes.

HILDA. I'm blind. Not like there's going to be an inspection. I could teach you. You could go to college.

CAMELIA. I'd never show. Less someone makes me.

HILDA. I'll make you. I'll be your monitor like 'inside'.

CAMELIA. You can't even see me.

HILDA. Your jailor, if you like… here with me. Day and night. Teach you all I know. And you can be my eyes…

CAMELIA. But you don't even know me.

HILDA. You'd have to work, mind. I'll teach you to bake, braise, broil, steam, simmer…

CAMELIA. You'll get fed up wiv me. Everyone does.

HILDA. There'll have to be rules. Curfews and whatnot.

CAMELIA. What about my freedom?

HILDA. Thought freedom was your problem.

CAMELIA. I can't live here. I just can't.

HILDA. Why not?

Pause. CAMELIA *can't trust her kindness.*

CAMELIA. You got no computer.

HILDA (*with exasperation*). So, you want to go back to that scum? Go on then. Clear off!

CAMELIA. I ain't stupid.

HILDA. I'm well aware of that.

CAMELIA. I'll mess wiv your head. I'm warning ya. You'll start wishin you was deaf as well as blind. I'll let you down. I always do.

HILDA. I reckon I'm good for just one more before I fold the final deckchair.

HILDA *approaches the door.*

Some little voice inside your head knows better than what you do.

HILDA *locks the door and puts the key down her bra.*

CAMELIA. Man! Where dem pills? Proper need one nah.

HILDA. I got some chocolate somewhere.

CAMELIA. I ain't a kid. (*Pause.*) Where is it?

HILDA. We'll make a routine so you know what's coming. Work and play. And like I say I'll teach you everything I know, starting with this.

She brandishes the potato peeler in one hand.

Or this.

She retrieves the doorkey from her bra in other hand.

You choose…

CAMELIA *approaches her, hesitates… she chooses the key.*
She approaches the door. Stops.

CAMELIA. If I wasn't so fuckin hungry I'd be able to think
    straight.

Scene Four

CAMELIA (*to us*). Mum proper hated gettin on the bus wiv us.
    We'd go visit Auntie Jolie, her sister, Tottenham. Had to be
    when her husband weren't there cos he never liked our mum.
    I don't know why. So we're all togevva on da bus an Otis
    hits Destiny wiv his Game Boy so she won't stop cryin, and
    Mum don't know how to shut her up. So, dis man on the bus
    wiv like the longest beard I ever saw yeah, he comes over
    and gives da kids a toffee and then he give us all one and
    then he like leaves us the whole bag. And my mum starts
    cryin. And she won't have no toffees or play wiv her phone
    or nuffink. She just cries all the way, till she gets a call from
    Troy… then she's like, 'We gotta get off an get the next bus
    back right away.' So we never even get to Auntie Jolie's.
    Proper shame cos she's got dis rabbit in her back yard da
    kids like to mess wiv. Me as well yeah. Gonna get a rabbit
    one day when I get a garden. They can come round to mine
    then. Yeah, come round to mine.

Lights down on CAMILIA. *Up on* HILDA.

HILDA (*to us*). We'd been married a while, me and Ted. I
    wanted a family. We both did but somehow it never
    happened. So I got all excited when the new family-planning
    clinic opened, off the high street. Without telling Ted, I took
    myself along, expecting them to help me get myself
    pregnant. Plan my family like it said on the posters. I was so

disappointed when it was all about the opposite. Young gels lucky enough to conceive so easily they had to find ways to stop themselves. I don't know what I was expecting really. Magic? Some sort of answer to our bad luck in bed. I knew I wasn't alone but that didn't stop me from feeling like I was. Applied for a job turning out school dinners. Worse budget I'd ever come across but I did what I could. Half three I stayed on to play football with the juniors. They let me in goal. Sometimes the parents were late picking up their kids, so I'd take em home, and give em their tea. That's how it started. I taught them how to make fudge and knit. Even the boys. Course I was on at Ted to adopt, but he wasn't havin any of it, so I put forward to foster. Ted never loved them like I did. He couldn't fathom where I got that from. My love for kids who weren't my own.

Blackout.

Lights up on HILDA's *kitchen/living area. Summer.* CAMELIA, *with a basket of ironing, speaks on the landline.*

CAMELIA. No... granddaughter... you been sayin dat for three months a coat of paint wouldn't kill ya... just cos she can't see don't... well, I'll have to get my lawyer make hisself known to ya... you get me... Good... an tell em bring ID.

She replaces the phone. Closes her eyes as she makes her way back to the ironing, pretending to be blind. Mobile rings. She answers with a different attitude.

You ain't seen me, don't believe ya... He's my driving instructor! Yeah proper lessons... I ain't shellin out... Hilda, what I live wiv... I told ya, Zach, I ain't got it... throwed it in da canal... Don't care if you don't... I ain't got it no more!

She rings off and turns up Spanish music full blast. She finds the blue plastic bag under the sofa. Carefully she puts it in the swing bin as the music crescendos, so that she doesn't hear HILDA *enter. She jumps when she turns.*

You early. Never heard your minibus.

HILDA. Not surprised.

CAMELIA *turns the music down… we see* HILDA*'s hair has been restyled to make her look younger.*

Still a load of crap is it?

CAMELIA. 'Salright for background.

HILDA *takes off her cardigan impatiently.* CAMELIA *sets up the ironing board to work.*

What's wrong? Dey never cancel flamenco again?

HILDA. Carlos has gone back to hairdressing. The new teacher wants us dancing in pairs! I want to dance on my own. That's what I love about it. There's never enough men to go round anyway. Not that I care if it's Norman or Audrey I bump in to.

CAMELIA. I'll come wiv ya next time. Tell her she's teachin solo or else. You want a cuppa?

HILDA. No thanks. Rufus on security is leaving so Doreen set up a tea party in the garden. They're my friends right, so you'd think they'd of cottoned on by now. I know all their voices, and I remember their faces. Every wrinkled inch. So they're all outside in the garden nattering, only as I start walking towards them to join in, they grow silent on me. All of them clam up! How do I know where they are if they stop talking? I can feel them all staring at me like I'm another creature to them now. Wish they could be normal with me like you.

CAMELIA. You know what you wanna do? Pray. All ol ladies should. I pray for ya every night. Arks him to bring back your sight.

HILDA. He can't help me.

CAMELIA. He can. Dat's da point of him.

HILDA. He can't! You hear me. I am never going to see again. Ever!

Pause as HILDA *blows her nose.*

Before I forget, Mick the driver's going to give you a lesson in the minibus Friday.

CAMELIA. Serious?

HILDA. He likes you. They all do. You could get a job there one day.

CAMELIA. Reckon one ol lady's enough for me.

CAMELIA *'s mobile rings but she ignores it.*

HILDA. You going to get that?

CAMELIA. It's Alice my social. She's goin mental over me.

CAMELIA *retrieves the plastic bag from the bin but she doesn't know where to put it.*

HILDA. Invite her over, gel. Then she'll see for herself how well you're doing.

CAMELIA. Nah. She'll start crying like loads of snot, I'm tellin ya.

HILDA *gets up and moves towards her.* CAMELIA *moves away from her, holding the bag awkwardly. Something drops from the bag. A neat firearm.* CAMELIA *picks up the gun.*

HILDA. What was that?

CAMELIA. Knocked an ashtray innit. You wanna get rid of em. Listen, Hilda. Today I made a decision.

CAMELIA *hides the gun in the bottom of the fruit bowl, gets back to ironing.*

I'm gonna be a taxi driver.

HILDA. Steady on. You've only had three lessons.

CAMELIA. Loads more innit. My mate Dean, we was in care togevva. We'd sneak out like at three in the mornin. He used to hot-wire Japanese motors off the street and we'd take off, like all over Essex where he was born.

HILDA. You still in touch with him?

CAMELIA. Nah. He looked like a potato an he stole all my vouchers.

CAMELIA's *mobile alerts her with a text. She reads it but talks to* HILDA *at the same time to distract her.*

Hilda, you gotta have a go at next door yeah. Her cat craps like all over your yard.

HILDA. She's from Bulgaria, she won't understand.

CAMELIA. I could bang it into her. I nearly trod on some hangin out da washin. An like for you, it's gotta be even worser.

HILDA. No such thing as worser.

CAMELIA. I seen loads worser. These knickers of yours gonna frighten that cat away if we lucky.

CAMELIA's *mobile bleeps with another text. She keeps talking while she moves the gun from the fruit bowl. Looks around and puts it in a cupboard.* HILDA *puts on an apron.*

You gone an hid dem biscuits?

HILDA. There's fruit in the bowl. You had eight biscuits yesterday.

CAMELIA. What? Sometimes I think you're just pretendin to be blind to get attention.

HILDA *laughs ironically as she assembles dinner things.*

HILDA. That's right. It's so much more of a laugh with all the bleeps and clicks and murmurs in my life. Before I could rustle up an apple pie in half an hour and now it takes me all day. All day.

CAMELIA. You could have it easy but you don't. Dey got pies down Londis. Why d'ya give yourself da mission?

CAMELIA *blocks the cupboard area from* HILDA.

What? I'll get it for ya.

HILDA. Mustard. We're doing Welsh rarebit remember?

CAMELIA *removes mustard and gun. Gives mustard to* HILDA.

Call it what you like but the satisfaction I get from the 'doing' is as good as the taste. The day I eat a shop-bought pie you can take me out and shoot me.

CAMELIA *hesitates. Puts the gun in a drawer.*

CAMELIA. You proper blame me for not changin my habits an you're like twice as bad. You can eat your face off Nando's for nuffink but you won't even try it. I don't get it. If you was broke, you wouldn't be shellin out for my drivin lessons.

HILDA *takes off apron emphatically.*

HILDA. Go on then. Get your cardi, and mine. Let's go and find your Nando's.

CAMELIA. Serious?

HILDA. We could meet Alice there. Where is it exactly?

CAMELIA *goes to fetch cardigans but a text comes through that stops her.*

CAMELIA. You know what, I'm like proper tired tonight. Anuvver time yeah.

HILDA. We can eat here, then get the 14, down the South Bank. Have an ice cream by the river.

CAMELIA. Why would I ever wanna go there?

HILDA. You live in London and you've never been to the Thames?

CAMELIA. I seen it on da news. In da background.

HILDA. What about Big Ben? The Houses of Parliament?

CAMELIA. I ain't no fuckin tourist. Let's stay in, fix your rarebit. I got a headache comin on.

CAMELIA *looks out of the window. Nervous.* HILDA *faces her. Serious.*

HILDA. You promised me you'd cut yourself off from them good and proper.

CAMELIA. I am I swear. It's Alice. I'll text her I've gone Jamaica.

HILDA. They've got your passport. Just tell her you're staying with your nan.

CAMELIA. She knows my nan lives Romania wiv her new boyfriend. She knows all about me. She could do me on *Mastermind*, cept no one would watch. How come you never had no kids of your own?

HILDA. You slice the loaf… I'll grate the cheese.

HILDA *prepares the meal, with* CAMELIA *helping*.

Before I married I had a child.

CAMELIA. You never?

HILDA. I was sixteen and green. He was married.

CAMELIA. Who's the slapper now!

HILDA. I never called you a slapper and I never will. What happened to you was not your fault.

CAMELIA. You love him?

HILDA. He was dapper, different, or so I thought. We were staff together, a country club. Sporty types with cars to match. We used to watch them arriving from the basement kitchen window. He used to lift me up for a better view. Dropped me like a hot coal when I told him I was pregnant. I couldn't keep him on my own, not on my wages.

CAMELIA. What? You give him away?

HILDA *nods*.

What about your benefits?

HILDA. We could have both starved. His new mum wrote me letters, for the first year.

CAMELIA. How could ya?

HILDA. I reckon we should do away with family once and for all.

CAMELIA. What? Like everyone livin in care?

HILDA. Which is worse? Living at home or living in care?

CAMELIA. We was talkin about you. I'll lay the table yeah.

Something is posted through the letter box. HILDA *is alerted.*

More junk mail! Some curried pizza. Put it recyclin yeah?

CAMELIA *screws up the note, anxious. She gets the gun out of the drawer to find a better hiding place.*

HILDA. You better be straight with me, gel. Are you hiding drugs in my flat?

CAMELIA. No! I swear. My bruvver's crew… dey want somink offa me. But now I gone an spent it. We need spoons yeah?

HILDA. You give it back then they'll leave you alone? How much?

CAMELIA. Too much.

HILDA. Tell him. Tell all of them. They get their money if they agree to keep you out of it, for good.

HILDA *finds* CAMELIA. *She holds her face in her hands and pulls her close in towards her.* CAMELIA *holding the gun behind her back.*

You can trust me. You know that. Whatever it takes.

HILDA *kisses* CAMELIA *on the forehead.* CAMELIA*'s mobile rings. She breaks free, recognises the number, suddenly delighted.*

CAMELIA. It's Mum! I told you she would.

She stashes the gun back under the sofa as she answers the call.

…I wanna talk to her not you… Then wake her up… none of your fuckin business, Troy… let me talk to her now… Why what's happenin… Why didn't she tell me?

She hangs up. Slams down her mobile and grabs her jacket.

I'm goin out, get some chips.

HILDA. Dinner's ready. You get the plates.

CAMELIA *gets to the door and remembers she can't go out. Frustrated, she bangs her head against the door.*

CAMELIA. She's got anuvver one on da way. An I'm like the last one to know.

HILDA. They won't let her keep it.

CAMELIA. Shut up!

HILDA. She's messed up four of you and she's gonna do it again unless the social catch up with her. Plates!

CAMELIA *gets out two plates. Bringing them to* HILDA, *she stops, smashing them to the ground.* HILDA *calm.*

We'll eat it with our fingers then shall we?

Blackout.

Scene Five

HILDA (*to us*). Gary was seven when they asked him if he wanted to stay with us, his foster parents, or go back to his mum, he couldn't answer. Wouldn't answer. He was too scared to get it wrong. So they assumed kinship was best for him. His mum was going to turn herself round and win back her little boy. The same boy we'd been fostering for twenty-two months. (*Pause.*) He didn't live to see sixteen. Finished himself off in her bathroom, in case she might not notice otherwise. No note. Ted and I weren't family. No one told us what'd happened. We had to find out by chance. Maybe that's why I've lost my sight. You see, if ever I saw Gary's mother again, in the street, I don't think I could keep myself from finishing her off with my bare hands.

Lights change.

HILDA*'s kitchen/living area. Days later.*

Evidence of a break-in. Furniture turned over. We hear laughter, off. HILDA *and* CAMELIA *enter together with shopping.*

CAMELIA. Think of da time you wasted. I mean not even a keb…

CAMELIA *sees the state of the place and stops.*

HILDA. What? We forget something?

CAMELIA. Nah. Can we make chips again yeah? I need the practice.

CAMELIA *looks for the gun under the sofa. It has gone.*

HILDA. Not every night. We were christening the new hob that's all.

CAMELIA, *distraught, starts clearing the way for* HILDA *to reach her chair.*

CAMELIA. And who sorted that for ya?

HILDA. I don't want you doing stuff I can do myself. I'll end up a cabbage.

HILDA *goes to sit. Misses the chair and stumbles.* CAMELIA *helps her…*

Didn't I tell you not to move anything!

CAMELIA. I didn't. Didn't mean to. You gonna sit down or what?

HILDA *moves towards the kitchen as* CAMELIA *gets in her way.*

It's my cake. I made it, not you. You chill yeah.

The landline starts to ring.

You wanna get that?

HILDA *answers the phone*. CAMELIA *straightens the place*.

HILDA (*on phone*). Speaking… no, I'm quite sure… yes I am but I never asked for no dog… I'm not an idiot. Of course I didn't. I'd know if…

CAMELIA. What's the point of bein blind if you don't get a dog!

HILDA (*on phone*). I'm sure they are… I can manage without… really… and to you.

HILDA *puts down the phone*.

Don't you dare do anything like that again.

CAMELIA. They so well trained they would like die for ya. And you'd never like be on your own.

HILDA. You planning your escape?

CAMELIA. I never said dat. I like it here. Borin some of da time but…

HILDA. If you're hanging out with a blind woman just to get a dog off of her then you'd better clear off now!

CAMELIA. I'm makin you a cake! Never done that for no one. I'll get a dog of my own one day! Not like that stinkin bulldog Troy got. It ain't even his. He just lookin after it for some mate doin time. It went and bit my liccle sister's arm an Troy kicks it right across the room. So dumb it still come back for more.

HILDA *is on the move towards the bathroom*.

Where you goin?

HILDA. Powder my nose. You check the cake.

HILDA *exits to bathroom*. CAMELIA, *on mobile, whispers a message*.

CAMELIA. Look I know you come an got it, Zach. Pick up will ya!… I'm tellin Mum you got it so don't do nuffink stupid. You know what I'm sayin… Promise you won't go near Henry wiv it… Call me yeah.

She rings off as HILDA *emerges from the bathroom, sniffing the air.*

HILDA. Ready to come out I reckon.

CAMELIA *takes the cake out and puts it on the table. A perfect Victoria sponge.*

CAMELIA. Oh Hilda. I wish you could see it. It looks real.

HILDA. Course it's real. We should bring it down the centre tomorrow and share it out.

CAMELIA. Why?

HILDA. That's what you do with birthday cake. Show it off and share it out. You should be proud of yourself, gel.

CAMELIA. I wanna bring it to my mum. Proper loves cake when she's pregnant.

CAMELIA *looks for a cake tin.*

HILDA. What? What has that woman ever done for you?

CAMELIA *finds a tin and empties out biscuits.*

You promised you'd keep away from her. And her boyfriend.

CAMELIA. He ain't gettin none. Be jus the two of us.

CAMELIA *puts the cake in the tin.* HILDA *stands motionless.*

HILDA. Her birthday as well is it?

CAMELIA. Don't vex yourself. I'll make you anuvver one when I get back.

HILDA. No. I'm coming with you. Where's my stick?

CAMELIA. You can't! You'll slow me down.

HILDA. Tough! I'm your jailor. It's my job.

HILDA *goes to bar the front door.* CAMELIA *finds her bag.*

You've got your social worker coming five o'clock, to discuss access with your brother and sister.

CAMELIA. That ain't today? Shit! I'll call her change it.

HILDA. What about their foster family? You can't let everyone down! I won't let you.

CAMELIA. You can't stop me. I'll climb out the bathroom winda.

HILDA. No! Please, Camelia. You can't. You won't come back.

CAMELIA *puts on* HILDA*'s music.*

CAMELIA. Course I will. Listen to yer music yeah.

HILDA. If you don't know what you are to me...

CAMELIA. Anuvver time yeah.

CAMELIA *leaves by the bathroom window.* HILDA *shouts after her.*

HILDA. Tell her from me. Tell her I hope she chokes on it!

HILDA *alone with the flamenco music. With her back to the audience, she starts to move. She stamps both feet uncertainly, then with more force she moves further upstage. It's not a performance, it is a means of survival.*

Blackout.

Scene Six

Hours later. 4 a.m. CAMELIA *enters, stuffing her face with handfuls of cake from the tin.* HILDA *emerges, relieved.*

CAMELIA. You're the one meant to be in charge. You shoulda stopped me.

HILDA. Why wouldn't you answer your phone? Your social, Alice was here in tears warning you with messages not to go inside.

CAMELIA. She's always in tears. Cries about stuff before it even happens. Shouldn't be a social worker, she should be a fuckin fortune-teller.

HILDA *knocks over the cake tin.*

HILDA. Did you know about the court order to remove the baby?

CAMELIA. I'm the last person knows stuff. Some witch woman down the landin barks at me like it is my fault she's gonna sue the council. Like I must know where dey gone.

HILDA. They should be shot leaving a dog locked up like that.

CAMELIA. I was gonna walk straight back out, the stink was… like you can't imagine, but then I see all her shoes lined up down the end of the hall. I know she can't never last long wivout her shoes. So like I wasn't surprised, when I heard her. She was outside, proper vexed wiv some lippy neighbour givin her grief.

HILDA. Both of them?

CAMELIA. Troy musta been waitin in da van. The stink was still makin me wanna puke but I didn't want her to like suffer it, even though when you fink about it, it was her what made the stink, leavin da dog to die, but I reckon it was him not her… So dere she was, my mum, wiv her bump, right in front of me, arms full of empty bags. I knew she was never gonna fess up, takin off wivout tellin me, so I let it go, an I tell her I'm glad she come back and it's lucky I'm here cos I got stuff to tell her.

HILDA. What stuff?

CAMELIA. Then I show her the cake what I made and she sort of smiles and goes, 'That's nice, darlin, that's lovely that is.' So I said I'd get us tea yeah. She's gettin her shoes into de bags down the hall and I'm like lookin everywhere for the teapot and clean mugs but like nuffink is clean, an I gotta ice ma cake, so I start washin up but there's no liquid an no milk in this stinkin place an it's bare stupid me tryin to make it like it ain't, so I decide like we should go out yeah, café down the canal, eat my cake dere, outta da stink. So I go down the hall to tell her my plan only she must be in the bedroom findin more shoes cos I can't see her. Only she ain't in the bedroom, she ain't in the bathroom neither. The front door's still open and I hear anuvver voice yellin out she's gonna call da feds, so I go out and look over the railin to where this nutter neighbour's screamin 'n' pointin down... and there she is, wiv her bags full of shoes. She's put on a strappy pair so she can hardly walk, but she squeezes herself an her bump, between de parked cars and I shout down to her but she don't hear me and I know like there's no point. I'll never catch up wiv her.

HILDA. I'm glad they're taking the baby away.

CAMELIA. Shut up! She ain't like dat when she's clean.

HILDA. I'll be dancing Covent Garden before your mum cleans up.

CAMELIA. You never even met her!

HILDA. If I did I'd punch her lights out. You must tell Alice you've seen her.

CAMELIA. No. She won't harm it. She's never cruel.

HILDA. Worse than cruel. Her baby'll be born into a cold shivering craving. Screaming for something more than mother's milk... I've seen the incubators all lined up like your mum's shoes. She should be sterilised.

CAMELIA. You can't say that.

HILDA. Like the bitch she is!

CAMELIA. You can't have kids so no one else should! She's sick innit. She does stuff, says stuff she don't mean. What's your excuse?

HILDA. She doesn't care thrupence for you, gel, and she never will. Why can't you see it?

CAMELIA. She's my mum! You're just some bitter twisted old fanny never got what it wanted.

HILDA *grabs* CAMELIA *and slaps her hard across the face.*

HILDA. Get out!

HILDA *moves away to collect herself.*

CAMELIA. You can't just chuck us out.

HILDA. I wash my hands of you. Get your things and go.

CAMELIA. You can't. I'm havin a baby. (*Pause.*) You wanna like sit down.

HILDA. In all my life I've never felt less like sitting down.

CAMELIA. I thought I'd tell you on your birthday, like tomorrow, only I'm tellin you nah. So you can get used to it. Got five months to go innit. And I was gonna bake you anuvver cake I was. Get dem birthday candles down Londis but dey only come in packs of twenty and you're like nearly four packs so it proper rinses me...

HILDA. Who's the father?

CAMELIA *doesn't answer. Finds sherry.*

You never got to tell her, you can tell me. Put that bottle down!

CAMELIA. Dey was like all laughin. An Henry is filmin it. Me on da ground. It was my chance to like be sworn 'in' wiv em. (*Pause.*) Ma bruvver Zach, he like storms in an he smashes Henry's camera but that don't stop dem takin turns wiv me. (*Slugs sherry.*) Smell of petrol on da carpet in my face. Then dey put some bag over my head. Smelled of curry. I can't see but I can feel... Different ways they wannit... not lookin at me.

HILDA. They forced you?

CAMELIA. Never said dey couldn't.

HILDA. That's not the same as sayin they could. How many?

CAMELIA. Five.

HILDA. Jesus! When was this?

CAMELIA. Shame.

HILDA. Not yours, gel.

CAMELIA. Used to be my lucky number. From now on it gonna be two. They just plague me for some cash bitch. Dat's how I come to you da first time, robbed ya, stack some notes for em.

HILDA. Between my youth and yours we had something called feminism. I was never a big fan, but you… you let them treat you worse than yesterday's meat.

CAMELIA. Gotta forget what happen. Not my baby's fault his dad's some wasted gangsta. I ain't gonna tell. Even if it's a boy, he won't ever know how he started. I'll make somink up. You should be pleased for me. Hilda. You can be like godmuvver.

HILDA. You don't know how you will feel when it's born. It's no love-child.

CAMELIA. It's still my baby. We could do it togevva, Hilda. Look at all dem kids up on da walls. Leila says you was da best and dat's what I want.

HILDA. I could see them days.

CAMELIA. I'll like bring it out, feed da ducks when you wanna bit of peace yeah.

HILDA *moves towards her.*

HILDA. Before you rush into things, let me bring you along to the doctor, talk through your options.

CAMELIA. I'm havin it. An it's gettin da best yeah. No charity shit, or car-boot bollocks, an the best jars they got. I'll keep it warm in the winter and cool in the summer. And I'll take it to the zoo. Mash up bananas. Bring it down the clinic, do them checks they do, so it's got a proper record like, if it's ever sick, but it won't be.

CAMELIA *stares at* HILDA *for some response.*

HILDA. The one thing that baby needs is the one thing you can't give it, cos you don't know it yourself.

CAMELIA. Now you're gassin.

HILDA. I'm gonna say this once. Please consider adoption. For both your sakes.

CAMELIA. Serious? No one does that no more. Not unless dey in da loony bin. Be pleased for me, Hilda. I'm havin a little baby to love and...

HILDA. Love it the way your mum loves you? It's a verb. A doing word.

CAMELIA. You and your fuckin words. Leave her outta dis. First time in my life somink good is happenin. I thought you'd wanna share it.

HILDA. There's folk out there, real grown-ups, would give your baby a great start in life.

CAMELIA. But it's my baby! Mine!

HILDA. No! You give birth to it. Give not take. Give give give...

CAMELIA. You want me to do what you done?

HILDA. Wait!

CAMELIA. You got a hole in your heart you ain't never gonna fill. An thinkin dat what you done was right don't make dat hole go away. And now, you want da same for me. Well, thanks a lot, Hilda. I'm outta here. Happy fuckin birthday!

Blackout.

Scene Seven

HILDA (*to us*). I wasn't Catholic or anything but the nuns never
seemed to mind. They took good care of me before he was
born and after. They didn't even make me pray which always
surprised me. He had jet-black hair, like a tinker, one of the
nuns laughed about that. They were rude about his ears 'n'
all. Perhaps they didn't know I could hear. They let me hold
him for a bit. Say goodbye. There was no hello. A couple of
months after Ted died I thought I'd try to track him down.
My boy. Didn't even know his proper name but the Mother
Superior wrote me back she'd pass on my letter. Waited
months, a year. Never heard nothing back. When I wrote
again, they just said there's been no comment. I reckon that
means he's having a good life. Why mess that up? Only I
keep thinking he might change his mind, just out of curiosity.
Those big ears. Hope he's grown into them.

Lights change.

HILDA*'s kitchen/living area. Months later.*

HILDA *is closing the door. Her leg is bandaged.* CAMELIA
*is parking a high baby pram, laden with shopping
underneath.*

(*To* CAMELIA.) How long have you been waiting out there?
Why didn't you knock?

CAMELIA. I was like passin so I thought… yeah, then I
thought…

HILDA. Good to see you. Can I give her a cuddle?

CAMELIA. She's sleeping yeah. Makes a change. What's
happening wiv that oven I got ya?

HILDA. Bit of an accident boiling an egg.

CAMELIA. Fuck's sake, man!

HILDA. It was one of them days. Then the hospital goes and
alerts the social who alerts my next of kin so…

CAMELIA. Next of what?

HILDA. My goddaughter Ruth, climbs on her high horse, and gets the social to rip out my oven. But I got Lorraine back tea times, so they're leaving me alone, for now. Do you need money?

CAMELIA *starts wandering.*

CAMELIA. No. You buy dog biscuits by mistake?

HILDA. Start our training April.

CAMELIA. That ain't fair! Labrador?

HILDA. And from what the trainer tells me he's more intelligent than me. They say they're monitoring him now for bad behaviour and if there's any 'history' they pick up on it straight away. Is there something you need?

CAMELIA *goes to take the brake off the pram.*

CAMELIA. This ain't right. Should never of come.

HILDA. Please stay a bit. Give yourself a break while she's napping…

HILDA *finds* CAMELIA *and holds her arm.*

What is it, Camelia?

CAMELIA *breaks away. She gets out fags but doesn't light up.*

Heard from Leila you got yourself a flat. Said she was jealous you got a balcony.

CAMELIA. What else did she tell ya?

HILDA. About your brother Zach. I'm so sorry.

CAMELIA. If he'd only waited a few days he'd of seen my baby an he might of changed his mind.

HILDA. You should have come to see me then. It can't have been easy…

CAMELIA. You made yourself proper clear las time what you didn't want.

HILDA. Maybe I was wrong.

CAMELIA's mobile rings. She answers, moving away.

CAMELIA. Yeah… I did but they didn't pick up… well she's lyin… course I wanna come… I told ya… I'll be there. I will.

During this, HILDA *goes to the pram. She carefully puts her hands in to feel the baby's head. Nothing but shopping.*

HILDA. You bring the pram here to trick me?

CAMELIA. Pram's all I got left. But I ain't givin up on her, I swear.

HILDA. Tell me she's not been harmed?

CAMELIA. What d' you care? You wanted me to give her away!

HILDA *pulls* CAMELIA *round to face her.*

HILDA. Where is she? Tell me exactly where your baby is.

CAMELIA. Wiv a foster-carer till my case comes up. I see her three times a week at the family centre Tottenham. It's a mission on da bus, an it proper wrecks me inside. I couldn't believe it when dey come and took her away, Hilda. You the only person knows what I'm like inside. My solicitor says you're my best bet.

HILDA. Does he?

CAMELIA. She. You don't even know what got me in dis mess! Fuckin bitch. They took her side cos she was like nearly at the end of her trainin so they…

HILDA. What training?

CAMELIA. I got put in da mother-an-baby unit for…

HILDA. But Leila said you got a flat.

CAMELIA. She's anuvver fuckin cow! Thought she was meant to be my mate. No one, like no one told me what it was gonna be like on my own. Then I got the feds comin round tellin me stuff about Zach, like they was lettin Henry off da case fer shooting him cos they ain't got nuffink on him. Like dey know fer a fact Henry's a drug-dealin psycho, pervert gangsta... But dey don't care about dat. He never shot my bruvver. Zach done it hisself. So like I proper needed to get off my face. Just for one night. I didn't know she was gonna wake up.

HILDA. You didn't leave her alone?

CAMELIA. We was always on our own when Mum worked nights. No one said nuffink... So da first time dey found out, da social was like cool wi me...

HILDA. You did it again?

CAMELIA. What was I sposed to do? Bring her wiv me?

CAMELIA *smashes her fist on the table*.

I jus needed a night out. Is dat so terrible? I didn't mean to get trolleyed, but dere was dis crowd I used to hang wiv an... well... it got later dan I thought yeah and she musta had a tooth comin so she starts cryin... and when I get back it all kicks off. Da feds are dere wiv da social and they won't lissen to me. Say stuff to me like I'm high when I ain't.

HILDA. They take her into care?

CAMELIA. They give me a chance. I got a twelve-week programme in dis muvver-an-baby home. Proper supervised an dat.

HILDA. You don't know how lucky you are.

CAMELIA. An I done everyfink like dey said. Learnt loads about babies. Bet I know more 'n' you do. If only dat little witch Zoe hadn't offered to babysit while I straightened my hair. Later yeah, she goes to da uvver gals dat my baby ain't makin proper eye contact or like gettin enough 'stimulation'. So I jumped on her an give her some. She made such a fuckin fuss, head of staff goes to me... I am a risk to all of them, includin my, my own...

CAMELIA *fighting tears*.

And that's a fuckin lie. I would rather cut off dis arm than hurt her.

She grabs HILDA*'s hands holds them tight.*

Dey give my baby a guardian yeah, and a lawyer but if she could talk for herself, if only she could talk …

HILDA. She'd be just like you. Sticking up for Mum no matter what.

CAMELIA. This ain't about her!

HILDA. She get to keep her baby? Maybe you got the same solicitor!

CAMELIA. I don't see her no more.

HILDA. Allelujah!

CAMELIA. I got a case see, against the local authority, if they goin for adoption which dey are but, solicitor finks dere's like a chance I can like get my baby back. If I make some promises an someone, like you, what proper knows me, stands up in court and says like positive stuff about my character. (*Pause.*) They will listen to you, Hilda.

HILDA. Will they listen when I tell them your baby is better off without you.

CAMELIA *goes to pram, releases brake.*

CAMELIA. I knew you'd say that. After all I done for ya.

HILDA. Wait! Don't go. We can start where we left off. You and me.

CAMELIA. What?

HILDA. Give her up now without a fight. Let her go, Camelia. Once she's eighteen she can contact you again.

CAMELIA. And what if she don't?

HILDA. Make it easy now with the authorities and they'll make it easy on you. You can both get to know each other as adults. You'll only be thirty-six. You'll have years together, without the bit that will cripple you now. She'll thank you for it.

CAMELIA. She'll hate me for it.

HILDA. You don't know that.

CAMELIA. Why do you think your son never made contact?

Pause.

You give up on him. He ain't never gonna forgive dat.

HILDA. Wait. If you change your mind. Your room is still waiting.

CAMELIA. You don't get me. How can you when you is so full of 'right'. Always right, Hilda. I'm surprised you don't shit gold but I know you don't cos I've seen it. Close up. When you needed help.

HILDA. You've been good to me. I would never say otherwise.

CAMELIA. Right again. Don't you get sick of yourself?

HILDA. All the time! Since you left there's been a hungry hole that no one can fill. Not even a Labrador. I wake up in the morning and you're in my head like an irritating pop song I can't seem to shift. I miss you something chronic.

CAMELIA. Whose fault is that? What if I was your granddaughter yeah. Proper fam.

HILDA. I only care what is best for the kid.

CAMELIA. Dat's a bare lie! You tellin me you wouldn't stick up for me an save your blud? If I was your blud? You tellin me you wouldn't do anyfink you could to keep da baby in da basket after what you done before? But I ain't your blud.

HILDA. I can't lie for you in court. I can't. I can't even wish you luck. You need a darn sight more than that to bring up a child.

CAMELIA *moves the pram.*

Before you go, will you take the dolls? Please, the Russian dolls. I'd like you to have them.

CAMELIA. I don't want nuffink o' yours.

HILDA. For your daughter then.

CAMELIA *goes over to the Russian dolls and swipes them off the shelf. They roll all over the floor.*

CAMELIA. I never really liked em. Must of been pretendin like you.

CAMELIA *leaves with the pram.*

HILDA *gets on her knees searching for the dolls as the lights fade.*

End.

www.nickhernbooks.co.uk

facebook.com/nickhernbooks

twitter.com/nickhernbooks